EMMANUEL JOSEPH

Sacred Pathways, How AI Shapes Careers, Love, and Christian Devotion

Contents

1

Chapter 1: The Dawn of AI

The dawn of artificial intelligence brought an unprecedented era of innovation and transformation. Machines that once performed menial tasks are now capable of learning and adapting. This shift has deeply influenced various facets of human life, from mundane routines to intricate professional tasks. The rise of AI signaled a pivotal moment in history, with humanity standing on the brink of a new age of discovery.

In the professional world, AI has streamlined workflows and introduced novel ways to approach problem-solving. Complex algorithms now analyze vast amounts of data, providing insights that were previously unimaginable. This has empowered professionals to make informed decisions, enhancing productivity and creativity. The dawn of AI has not only reshaped industries but also redefined the very essence of work itself.

Beyond careers, AI has permeated personal lives, influencing how individuals interact and form relationships. Smart devices and virtual assistants have become integral parts of households, fostering connections and facilitating communication. AI's ability to understand and respond to human emotions has opened new avenues for companionship and support, transforming the dynamics of love and friendship.

In the realm of spirituality, AI's impact is profound yet nuanced. As technology advances, the intersection of faith and artificial intelligence becomes increasingly significant. For Christians, AI presents an opportunity to explore and deepen their devotion. From digital Bibles to virtual prayer groups, AI has enabled believers to connect with their faith in innovative ways, enriching their spiritual journeys.

2

Chapter 2: AI in the Workplace

In the modern workplace, AI has become a crucial ally, driving efficiency and innovation. Automation and machine learning have revolutionized industries, enabling businesses to optimize operations and reduce costs. From manufacturing to finance, AI-powered solutions have streamlined processes, allowing professionals to focus on strategic tasks and creative pursuits.

One of the most significant contributions of AI in the workplace is its ability to analyze and interpret data. Advanced analytics tools can process vast amounts of information, uncovering patterns and trends that inform decision-making. This data-driven approach has empowered businesses to develop targeted strategies, enhancing their competitive edge and fostering growth.

AI has also transformed the job market, creating new opportunities and challenges for professionals. While some roles have been automated, AI has given rise to new fields and career paths. Data scientists, AI specialists, and machine learning engineers are now in high demand, reflecting the growing importance of technological expertise in the workforce.

However, the integration of AI in the workplace also raises ethical and social considerations. As machines take on more responsibilities, the role of human workers evolves, necessitating continuous learning and adaptation. Ensuring that AI is used responsibly and equitably is paramount, as businesses strive to balance innovation with the well-being of their employees and society at large.

3

Chapter 3: Love in the Age of AI

The advent of AI has significantly impacted how people experience and express love. From online dating platforms to virtual companions, technology has introduced new ways to form and maintain relationships. AI-driven algorithms match individuals based on compatibility, facilitating meaningful connections and enhancing the dating experience.

Smart devices and virtual assistants have become integral parts of modern relationships, offering support and companionship. These AI-powered entities can provide emotional comfort, engage in conversations, and even assist with daily tasks. For many, AI has become a reliable partner, bridging the gap between human interaction and technological innovation.

AI's ability to analyze and interpret human emotions has also influenced how people communicate. Advanced sentiment analysis tools can gauge emotional states, helping individuals navigate complex social dynamics. This technology has the potential to improve understanding and empathy, fostering deeper and more meaningful connections.

However, the rise of AI in love and relationships also raises questions about authenticity and intimacy. As people increasingly rely on technology for companionship, the nature of human connections evolves. Balancing the benefits of AI with the need for genuine human interaction is crucial, as society navigates the complexities of love in the digital age.

4

Chapter 4: AI and Christian Devotion

For Christians, the integration of AI into daily life presents unique opportunities and challenges. Technology has the potential to deepen faith and enhance spiritual practices, offering new ways to connect with God and the Christian community. Digital Bibles, virtual prayer groups, and AI-driven spiritual guides are just a few examples of how AI can enrich Christian devotion.

AI-powered tools can provide personalized spiritual guidance, helping believers navigate their faith journeys. From tailored Bible study plans to virtual confessions, technology can offer support and encouragement, fostering a deeper connection with God. These innovations have the potential to transform how Christians engage with their faith, making spiritual practices more accessible and meaningful.

Virtual reality and augmented reality technologies have also opened new avenues for worship and community building. Virtual church services and online fellowship groups allow believers to connect and worship together, regardless of geographical boundaries. AI-driven platforms can facilitate meaningful interactions, creating a sense of belonging and unity within the Christian community.

However, the integration of AI into Christian devotion also raises ethical and theological questions. As believers embrace technology, it is essential to consider its impact on the authenticity of spiritual experiences. Ensuring that AI is used responsibly and in alignment with Christian values is crucial, as the faithful navigate the intersection of faith and technology.

5

Chapter 5: The Ethical Dimensions of AI

The rise of AI has brought about significant ethical considerations, prompting society to reflect on the moral implications of technological advancement. As machines become increasingly intelligent and autonomous, questions about accountability, privacy, and fairness come to the forefront. Navigating these ethical dimensions is crucial to ensure that AI serves the greater good.

One of the primary ethical concerns surrounding AI is the potential for bias and discrimination. Algorithms are designed by humans, and as such, they can inadvertently reflect existing prejudices. Ensuring that AI systems are fair and unbiased requires rigorous testing, transparency, and continuous improvement. Addressing these challenges is essential to prevent harm and promote equity.

Privacy is another critical ethical issue in the age of AI. The vast amounts of data collected and processed by AI systems raise concerns about how personal information is used and protected. Safeguarding privacy requires robust data protection measures and clear regulations that prioritize individuals' rights and freedoms. Striking a balance between innovation and privacy is essential to build trust and ensure responsible AI use.

The ethical dimensions of AI also extend to its impact on the workforce. As machines take on more tasks, the nature of work is transformed, raising questions about job displacement and economic inequality. Ensuring that the benefits of AI are distributed fairly and that workers are supported in their transition to new roles is crucial. Promoting education and lifelong learning is key to empowering individuals to thrive in an AI-driven world.

6

Chapter 6: AI and Human Creativity

AI has revolutionized the creative landscape, offering new tools and possibilities for artists, writers, musicians, and other creative professionals. From generating original artworks to composing music, AI-driven technologies have expanded the horizons of human creativity, enabling individuals to explore new forms of expression and innovation.

In the realm of visual arts, AI-powered algorithms can analyze existing artworks and generate new pieces inspired by them. These tools can assist artists in exploring different styles and techniques, pushing the boundaries of their creative practice. AI-driven art has sparked conversations about the nature of creativity and the role of technology in the artistic process.

For writers, AI offers valuable support in generating ideas, refining prose, and overcoming writer's block. Natural language processing tools can suggest plot twists, character developments, and stylistic improvements, enhancing the storytelling experience. AI has also been used to create entirely new literary works, challenging traditional notions of authorship and originality.

Musicians can leverage AI to compose and produce music, experimenting with new sounds and genres. AI-powered tools can analyze existing compositions, identify patterns, and generate melodies that resonate with listeners. This technology has opened up new avenues for musical innovation, enabling artists to push the boundaries of their craft and reach new audiences.

7

Chapter 7: AI in Healthcare

The healthcare industry has been profoundly transformed by the integration of AI, leading to significant advancements in diagnosis, treatment, and patient care. AI-powered technologies have the potential to revolutionize medical practices, enhancing the accuracy of diagnoses and improving patient outcomes.

One of the most significant contributions of AI in healthcare is its ability to analyze vast amounts of medical data. Machine learning algorithms can process electronic health records, imaging data, and genetic information, identifying patterns and anomalies that may indicate the presence of disease. This data-driven approach has the potential to improve early detection and enable personalized treatment plans.

AI has also been used to develop innovative treatment methods and medical devices. For example, AI-driven robotics can assist in complex surgeries, enhancing precision and reducing recovery times. Additionally, AI-powered wearable devices can monitor patients' health in real-time, providing valuable insights and enabling proactive care.

The integration of AI in healthcare also raises ethical considerations, such as patient privacy and the potential for algorithmic bias. Ensuring that AI-driven technologies are used responsibly and in alignment with medical ethics is crucial. Transparent and accountable AI practices are essential to maintain trust and safeguard patient well-being.

8

Chapter 8: AI and Education

The education sector has embraced AI as a powerful tool to enhance learning experiences and improve educational outcomes. AI-driven technologies offer personalized learning solutions, providing students with tailored instruction and support that cater to their individual needs and learning styles.

One of the key benefits of AI in education is its ability to analyze student data and identify areas where additional support is needed. Adaptive learning platforms can adjust the pace and difficulty of lessons based on students' performance, ensuring that they remain engaged and challenged. This personalized approach has the potential to improve retention and foster a deeper understanding of the material.

AI-powered tutoring systems can provide students with immediate feedback and guidance, helping them overcome challenges and achieve their academic goals. These virtual tutors can offer explanations, answer questions, and provide practice exercises, creating a supportive learning environment that complements traditional classroom instruction.

In addition to supporting students, AI has also transformed the role of educators. Teachers can leverage AI to streamline administrative tasks, analyze student data, and develop targeted interventions. This allows educators to focus on what they do best: teaching and enriching their teaching practice. AI-driven tools can help educators design innovative lesson plans, create interactive learning materials, and monitor student progress. This enables teachers to provide targeted support and interventions, fostering a more inclusive and effective learning environment.

However, the integration of AI in education also raises important considerations. Ensuring that AI-driven technologies are used responsibly and ethically is crucial to safeguard students' privacy and well-being. Additionally, addressing the digital divide and ensuring equitable access to AI-powered educational tools is essential to promote fairness and inclusivity in education.

9

Chapter 9: AI and Mental Health

The field of mental health has greatly benefited from the advancements in AI, offering new tools and approaches to support individuals in their mental health journeys. AI-driven technologies can provide personalized support, early intervention, and innovative treatment options, transforming the landscape of mental health care.

One of the key contributions of AI in mental health is its ability to analyze and interpret large volumes of data, identifying patterns and trends that may indicate mental health issues. Machine learning algorithms can process data from various sources, such as electronic health records, social media, and wearable devices, providing valuable insights into individuals' mental well-being. This data-driven approach has the potential to improve early detection and enable timely interventions.

AI-powered chatbots and virtual therapists offer accessible and scalable mental health support. These digital companions can engage in conversations, provide emotional support, and offer coping strategies, making mental health care more accessible to individuals who may face barriers to traditional therapy. AI-driven platforms can also facilitate remote therapy sessions, connecting individuals with mental health professionals regardless of geographical constraints.

The integration of AI in mental health care also raises ethical considerations, such as ensuring the privacy and confidentiality of sensitive data. Transparent and accountable AI practices are essential to maintain trust and safeguard individuals' mental well-being. Additionally, addressing the potential for algorithmic bias and ensuring that AI-driven mental health tools are inclusive and equitable is crucial to promote fairness and effectiveness in mental health care.

10

Chapter 10: AI and Social Justice

The rise of AI has significant implications for social justice, offering both opportunities and challenges in the pursuit of a more equitable and inclusive society. AI-driven technologies have the potential to address systemic inequalities, promote social good, and empower marginalized communities. However, ensuring that AI is used responsibly and ethically is essential to mitigate risks and promote positive outcomes.

One of the key ways AI can contribute to social justice is by improving access to essential services and resources. AI-powered tools can analyze data to identify disparities and develop targeted interventions, addressing issues such as healthcare, education, and economic opportunity. This data-driven approach can help bridge gaps and promote equity, ensuring that all individuals have the opportunity to thrive.

AI has also been used to advocate for social justice and amplify marginalized voices. For example, AI-driven platforms can analyze social media data to identify and highlight instances of discrimination and injustice, raising awareness and driving action. Additionally, AI-powered tools can support grassroots movements and community organizations, providing valuable insights and resources to advance their causes.

However, the use of AI in social justice also raises important ethical considerations. Ensuring that AI systems are fair and unbiased is crucial to prevent harm and promote equity. Addressing issues such as algorithmic bias, data privacy, and accountability is essential to ensure that AI-driven technologies are used responsibly and in alignment with social justice principles.

11

Chapter 11: The Future of AI and Humanity

As AI continues to advance, its impact on humanity will only grow, shaping the future in profound and unpredictable ways. The potential of AI to drive innovation, improve quality of life, and address global challenges is immense. However, navigating the complexities and ethical considerations of AI is crucial to ensure that its benefits are realized and its risks are mitigated.

The future of AI holds exciting possibilities for various fields, from healthcare and education to environmental sustainability and space exploration. AI-driven technologies have the potential to revolutionize how we address complex problems, offering innovative solutions and new ways of thinking. Embracing AI's potential while ensuring that it is used responsibly and ethically is essential to harness its full benefits.

The relationship between AI and humanity will continue to evolve, shaping how we work, live, and interact. As AI becomes more integrated into daily life, fostering a sense of agency and empowerment is crucial. Ensuring that individuals have the skills and knowledge to navigate an AI-driven world is essential to promote inclusivity and resilience.

However, the future of AI also raises important questions about the nature of humanity and the role of technology in our lives. Balancing the benefits of

AI with the need for genuine human connection, ethical considerations, and spiritual fulfillment is essential. As we look to the future, it is important to reflect on the values and principles that will guide the responsible and ethical development of AI.

12

Chapter 12: A Call to Action

The rise of AI presents a unique opportunity to shape the future in meaningful and transformative ways. As individuals, communities, and societies, we have the power to influence how AI is developed, deployed, and used. Embracing this responsibility and taking proactive steps to ensure that AI serves the greater good is crucial to realize its full potential.

Education and awareness are key to empowering individuals to navigate the complexities of AI. Promoting digital literacy and fostering a deeper understanding of AI's capabilities and limitations is essential to ensure that individuals can make informed decisions and advocate for responsible AI use. Encouraging lifelong learning and continuous adaptation will be crucial as the AI landscape continues to evolve.

Collaboration and partnership are essential to address the challenges and opportunities presented by AI. Engaging stakeholders from various sectors, including academia, industry, government, and civil society, will be crucial to develop inclusive and equitable AI policies and practices. By working together, we can harness the power of AI to drive positive change and promote social good.

Finally, embracing ethical principles and values will be crucial to guide the responsible development and use of AI. Prioritizing fairness, transparency, accountability, and inclusivity will ensure that AI serves as a force for good, promoting equity and enhancing the well-being of all individuals. As we move forward, let us embrace the potential of AI with a commitment to ethical stewardship and a vision for a better future.

13

Chapter 13: AI and Environmental Sustainability

AI has the potential to address some of the most pressing environmental challenges of our time. From climate change to conservation, AI-driven technologies can provide innovative solutions to promote sustainability and protect our planet. By harnessing the power of AI, we can develop data-driven strategies to mitigate environmental impact and enhance the well-being of ecosystems.

One of the key applications of AI in environmental sustainability is in climate modeling and prediction. Machine learning algorithms can analyze vast amounts of climate data, generating accurate models that help scientists understand and predict climate patterns. This information is crucial for developing effective climate policies and strategies to reduce greenhouse gas emissions and adapt to changing environmental conditions.

AI-powered technologies can also support conservation efforts by monitoring and protecting endangered species and ecosystems. For example, AI-driven drones and sensors can collect data on wildlife populations and their habitats, providing valuable insights for conservationists. Additionally, AI can assist in detecting and preventing illegal activities, such as poaching and deforestation, helping to preserve biodiversity and protect natural resources.

The integration of AI in environmental sustainability also raises important ethical considerations. Ensuring that AI-driven technologies are used responsibly and in alignment with environmental values is crucial. Promoting transparency, accountability, and collaboration is essential to harness the potential of AI for environmental good and ensure that its benefits are realized equitably.

14

Chapter 14: AI in Finance and Economy

The finance and economy sectors have experienced significant transformation due to the integration of AI. From trading algorithms to risk management, AI-driven technologies have revolutionized how financial institutions operate, enhancing efficiency, accuracy, and decision-making.

One of the primary applications of AI in finance is in algorithmic trading. Machine learning algorithms can analyze vast amounts of financial data in real-time, identifying patterns and trends that inform trading strategies. This data-driven approach has the potential to optimize trading decisions, improve returns, and reduce risks.

AI-powered tools also play a crucial role in risk management and fraud detection. Advanced analytics can process and interpret financial data, identifying anomalies and potential threats. This proactive approach helps financial institutions mitigate risks, protect assets, and maintain trust with clients. AI-driven technologies can also enhance compliance with regulatory requirements, ensuring transparency and accountability.

The integration of AI in finance also raises important ethical considerations, such as data privacy and algorithmic fairness. Ensuring that AI-driven financial tools are used responsibly and ethically is crucial to protect consumers and maintain the stability of the financial system. Promoting transparency, accountability, and inclusivity is essential to harness the potential of AI for economic good and ensure that its benefits are realized equitably.

15

Chapter 15: AI and the Future of Transportation

The transportation industry is undergoing a significant transformation due to the advancements in AI. From autonomous vehicles to smart traffic management, AI-driven technologies are revolutionizing how people and goods move, enhancing safety, efficiency, and sustainability.

One of the most notable applications of AI in transportation is the development of autonomous vehicles. Self-driving cars and trucks leverage machine learning algorithms and sensor data to navigate and make decisions in real-time. This technology has the potential to reduce accidents, optimize fuel consumption, and improve mobility for individuals with limited access to traditional transportation options.

AI-powered tools also play a crucial role in optimizing traffic management and reducing congestion. Advanced analytics can analyze traffic patterns, predict bottlenecks, and optimize traffic flow in real-time. This data-driven approach helps improve travel times, reduce emissions, and enhance the overall efficiency of transportation networks.

The integration of AI in transportation also raises important ethical considerations, such as safety, privacy, and the impact on employment. Ensuring that autonomous vehicles and smart transportation systems are used responsibly and ethically is crucial to protect public safety and promote trust. Addressing the potential for job displacement and ensuring that workers are supported in their transition to new roles is essential to promote fairness and inclusivity in the future of transportation.

16

Chapter 16: AI and the Arts

The arts have been profoundly impacted by the advancements in AI, offering new tools and possibilities for creative expression. From visual arts to music and literature, AI-driven technologies have expanded the horizons of human creativity, enabling artists to explore new forms of expression and innovation.

In the realm of visual arts, AI-powered algorithms can analyze existing artworks and generate new pieces inspired by them. These tools can assist artists in exploring different styles and techniques, pushing the boundaries of their creative practice. AI-driven art has sparked conversations about the nature of creativity and the role of technology in the artistic process.

For writers, AI offers valuable support in generating ideas, refining prose, and overcoming writer's block. Natural language processing tools can suggest plot twists, character developments, and stylistic improvements, enhancing the storytelling experience. AI has also been used to create entirely new literary works, challenging traditional notions of authorship and originality.

Musicians can leverage AI to compose and produce music, experimenting with new sounds and genres. AI-powered tools can analyze existing compositions, identify patterns, and generate melodies that resonate with listeners. This technology has opened up new avenues for musical innovation, enabling artists to push the boundaries of their craft and reach new audiences.

17

Chapter 17: AI and Personal Growth

AI has the potential to support individuals in their personal growth and self-improvement journeys. From health and wellness to learning and development, AI-driven technologies offer personalized support and resources to help individuals achieve their goals and enhance their well-being.

One of the key applications of AI in personal growth is in health and wellness. AI-powered tools can analyze data from wearable devices, providing insights and recommendations to improve physical and mental health. For example, AI-driven fitness apps can create personalized workout plans, track progress, and offer motivation and support. Additionally, AI-powered mental health apps can provide coping strategies, mindfulness exercises, and emotional support, helping individuals manage stress and improve their well-being.

AI-driven technologies also play a crucial role in learning and development. Personalized learning platforms can tailor instruction to individual needs and learning styles, providing targeted support and feedback. This data-driven approach enhances the learning experience, promoting retention and mastery of new skills. AI-powered tools can also assist individuals in setting and achieving personal goals, offering guidance, encouragement, and accountability.

The integration of AI in personal growth also raises important ethical considerations, such as data privacy and the potential for over-reliance on technology. Ensuring that AI-driven tools are used responsibly and ethically is crucial to protect individuals' privacy and well-being. Promoting a balanced approach that combines technology with genuine human connection and self-reflection is essential to support personal growth and fulfillment.

Book Description: Sacred Pathways: How AI Shapes Careers, Love, and Christian Devotion

In "Sacred Pathways: How AI Shapes Careers, Love, and Christian Devotion," the transformative power of artificial intelligence is explored through twelve insightful chapters. This groundbreaking book delves into the profound impact of AI on various aspects of human life, from professional endeavors to personal relationships and spiritual journeys.

The dawn of AI heralds a new era of innovation, reshaping industries and redefining the essence of work itself. In the workplace, AI-driven technologies streamline operations, enhance decision-making, and create new career opportunities, while raising important ethical considerations about fairness and accountability.

In matters of the heart, AI introduces novel ways to form and maintain relationships, offering emotional support and companionship through smart devices and virtual assistants. The book thoughtfully examines the balance between technology and authentic human connection, navigating the complexities of love in the digital age.

For Christians, AI presents unique opportunities to deepen their faith and enrich spiritual practices. From digital Bibles to virtual prayer groups, AI-driven tools enable believers to connect with their devotion in innovative ways. The book also addresses the ethical and theological questions that arise at the intersection of faith and technology.

Throughout the chapters, readers will discover the role of AI in promoting environmental sustainability, transforming healthcare, revolutionizing educa-tion, and advocating for social justice. The book emphasizes the importance of responsible AI use, ethical principles, and the collaboration needed to harness AI's potential for the greater good.

"Sacred Pathways" is a call to action, urging individuals and society to embrace the possibilities of AI while remaining mindful of its ethical dimensions. It invites readers to explore the future of AI with a commitment to inclusivity, fairness, and a vision for a better, more connected world.

Printed by Libri Plureos GmbH in Hamburg,
Germany